Sunset

ideas for great

GARDEN
DECOR

By Cynthia Bix
and the Editors of Sunset Books

Sunset Books ∎ Menlo Park, California

Sunset Books

vice president and general manager:
Richard A. Smeby

editorial director:
Bob Doyle

production director:
Lory Day

art director:
Vasken Guiragossian

Staff for this book:

managing editor:
Suzanne Normand Eyre

copy editor and indexer:
Pamela Evans

photo researcher:
Tishana Peebles

production coordinator:
Patricia S. Williams

special contributors:
*Lisa Anderson, Bridget Biscotti
Bradley, Barbara Brown,
Jean Warboy*

art director:
Alice Rogers

computer production:
Linda Bouchard, Joan Olson

*Cover: Elements of garden decor are artfully blended
with plantings in a serene patio corner. Garden
design by Walda Pairon. Cover design by Vasken
Guiragossian. Photography by Harry Haralambou.*

Dress up your garden

These days, everyone's excited about integrating art, antiques, and flea market finds with hardscape and plantings in their gardens. If this appealing idea has caught your fancy too, you've come to the right place. In this brand-new book, you'll find a breathtaking array of ideas for decorating your own outdoor spaces. More than 285 color photographs show ornaments, decorative structures, and furnishings that will dazzle and inspire you. The first three chapters illustrate a wealth of wonderful ideas; the final chapter offers solid design advice to help you make the most of your treasures. Throughout, you'll find instructions for simple projects such as sand lanterns, colorful mosaic pavers, and birdbaths. So feast your eyes on these pages and get ready to dress up your garden with the ornaments and decor you love!

Garden designers, artists, gallery owners, and homeowners gave us plenty of advice and ideas for inclusion in this book. Special thanks go to R G Turner Jr., editor of *Pacific Horticulture*, for reading the manuscript, and to Duane Kelly, producer of the San Francisco and Seattle Flower & Garden Shows, for allowing us to photograph the show gardens. We'd also like to thank Randi Herman (Berkeley, California), David Lewis of Little and Lewis, Inc. (Bainbridge Island, Washington), Ben Rodefer of A New Leaf Gallery (Berkeley, California), and Sandra Silvestri of A. Silvestri Co. (San Francisco, California).

Design credits for specific photos throughout the book are listed on pages 110–111.

contents

express
yourself

AN EMBARRASSMENT OF RICHES awaits today's design-conscious gardeners seeking to enhance their outdoor environs. It seems that everywhere we turn we're offered objects and features designed to beautify our gardens and complement our plantings. Fountains spilling sparkling water, carved stepping-stones, mosaic-encrusted urns, and gazing globes of every hue are just a few of our temptations; the difficulty has become one of narrowing choices. And you may already own decor that you'd like to incorporate outdoors—a family heirloom in the form of a statue, a weathered wood plaque discovered at a garage sale. How do you combine these objects in your garden without producing a jumble?

Because decor does so much to give a garden its character, your own personality should be your guide, expressed through the ornamental elements you select. That's why you should choose only objects that you really love. If you are crazy about a piece—whether a silly ceramic animal or an elegant three-tiered stone fountain—it will be right for your garden because it reflects your taste.

Still, it's a challenge—or perhaps a kind of chicken-and-egg dilemma—to combine those personal choices with other garden elements such as plants, furnishings, and the hardscape of walks and walls. Sometimes you plant to complement an ornament; other times you purchase or make a piece to harmonize with the plantings you have. Some features, such as fountains and arbors, will be permanently sited; others, like pots, birdhouses, and some statuary, can be played with indefinitely, moved around from spot to spot to keep the garden fresh.

From this book you'll not only gain ideas galore (from more than 285 photos); you'll also learn how to integrate all the elements of exterior decor successfully, for a garden that's uniquely your own.

ARTFUL TOUCHES

WHAT KIND OF ORNAMENT LOOKS BEST in a garden? For some people, it's a weathered stone statue swathed in ivy; for others, a procession of brightly painted animal cutouts parading across the lawn. It may be fine contemporary sculpture in a garden "gallery" for you, a one-of-a-kind birdhouse or collection of antique tools for your neighbor. **IN STYLE, SPIRIT, AND MATERIALS,** nowadays there's a tremendous choice of garden decor. Ornaments are largely what give your garden individual character: many gardens have the same plantings in common, but decorative accents are applied with your own personal stamp. You may be a flea market aficionado or a fine art collector; or perhaps you yourself are an artist. As long as you place your selections thoughtfully in their settings, just about anything can make a pleasing and attractive garden ornament. **IN THIS CHAPTER,** we display a treasury of garden objets d'art, from antiques to abstract pieces, from mirrors to statuary. In each of five thematic sections, you'll find an array of ornaments related in spirit and style. Sprinkled throughout are easy do-it-yourself projects and useful advice. So browse among the pages to get an idea of just how many looks a garden can have.

artful touches

a touch
of whimsy

A GRAB BAG OF WONDERFUL, WHIMSICAL GARDEN ORNAMENTS awaits you on the next ten pages. In them, the emphasis is on a lighthearted approach to exterior decorating. You'll see everything from colorful scarecrows to funky found objects—not to mention a whole menagerie of animals created from ceramic, metal, and even living shrubbery. These photographs are meant to fire your imagination and perhaps induce giggles or guffaws along the way.

Ornaments such as these might have come into your possession in any number of ways. One may be something you inherited—say, Aunt Martha's stone frog—or a flea market find such as a picturesque old watering can you just couldn't resist. Or perhaps you were enchanted by a piece of folk art at a seaside artist's studio and simply had to take it home.

Once you've fallen for a piece, it's what you do with it in the garden that makes it your own. Do you tuck the frog statue among the leaves, as a reward for the alert observer? Or does it belong up on a pedestal for all to see? Are you one to scatter wildly colorful whirligigs among the flower borders, or do you prefer to arrange a careful composition of foliage, small sculptures, and pots? It's for you to decide. Presented in a unique and original way, even a pink plastic flamingo can look good— just look at the pair on page 13!

This bench is taken! A larger-than-life scholarly frog is sure to evoke a chuckle from garden visitors seeking a quiet reading corner.

An old dining room chair (above) takes on new life—literally— with a cushiony seat of sod. The delightfully original composition at right pairs a collection of bowling balls with handcrafted ceramic bamboo canes.

RUSTY CHARMS

Antique garden ornaments and furniture—as well as old buckets, fencing, and other utilitarian outdoor objects—were often made of iron. Over time, as they react with oxygen and moisture, iron objects acquire an earth-colored coating of rust. In some cases, these old

pieces may have been sealed or painted for rust protection. If so, you will see a combination of chipped paint— perhaps in several layers or colors—and rust on venerable survivors.

For many people, this only adds to the charm of old pieces. A weathered bench or watering can blends into some gardens with all the comfortable ease of an old friend, and the rust or chipped paint gives it an aura of authenticity that speaks of its history and function. If you like this aged look, you can simply leave the piece as is, or—to prevent further deterioration—coat it with a clear, rustproof spray. You may decide you don't want to use a weathered old chair or section of fencing for its original function; instead, you may opt to use it as a charming trellis, letting vines climb over it. But if you need that chair or fence to remain fully functional, you will want to preserve it as much as possible, to prevent its being weakened by rust.

If you want to "start fresh," you can strip the iron, either by having it professionally sandblasted or by removing the rust and paint with a steel brush and sandpaper. Then you have three options: you can leave the piece to rust anew naturally; you can spray-coat it with rustproof spray; or you can paint it. Each option will give you a different look, as well as a different degree of protection for your fragment of history.

Being in the doghouse is fun—and funny— when both poodle and house are outsize topiary creations made by growing ivy over moss-and-wire frames.

A wrought-iron snail inching its way along the top of a stone wall adds a subtle, small-scale accent to a garden corner.

Sunlight glances off the iridescent wings of a metal butterfly, adding a permanent touch of color and shine to this flower border.

What are they doing in OUR pond? Three cutout metal geese waddle beside a gleaming expanse of water occupied by a couple of real-life ducks.

Bright with colorful flounces and frills of nasturtiums, a genteel lady scarecrow presides over the garden with country hospitality.

Pot people take a rest with their clipping tools in this amusing garden vignette. The figures were created by wiring together ordinary terra-cotta pots in a variety of sizes; flowery "hair" grows from the topmost containers.

Real yard-art originals, these colorful, long-necked chain-and-spring sculptures look for all the world like surreal wildlife clanking toward the watering hole in search of a drink.

A charmingly painted wood folk-art figure is comfortably ensconced in a sunny clump of black-eyed Susans.

The graceful lines of a weathered column are set off by the ornate forms of bear's breech growing around its base. Displaying the column alone, rather than as a pedestal for another piece, gives it an intriguing air of mystery.

Faux animals are unmatched for adding whimsy to the garden. The cast-concrete pig on the left, slumbering beneath his patchwork quilt, looks the very picture of porcine repose (but don't leave that quilt out in the rain!). On the right, those icons of 1950s yard art, plastic flamingoes, take on new life in a quiet, naturalistic pond setting.

Conversing among the foxgloves, faces fabricated from metal have a contemporary feel that makes an interesting contrast to the old-fashioned flowers.

This man in the moon's swirly, stylized form makes a lovely foil for surrounding flowers and foliage.

*Weathered vintage gasoline pumps
have traded their jobs at the filling
station for a secluded garden
corner lush with pampas grass and
fragrant wisteria.*

*A simple spiral of
rusted metal (top)
becomes garden art
when set into a vibrant
bed of mixed peren-
nials and annuals.
Beneath it, an old
pair of boots sprouts
hen and chicks from
top to toe.*

*A vignette of found
objects and plantings
poses intriguing ques-
tions. What, exactly, is
that white sphere half
hidden among the
foliage, and what
stories could the rusty
old upended trunk tell
of its travels?*

An original work in steel, this heart-shaped art piece, partnered with soft-textured pampas grass, has been allowed to rust so that it resembles a time-weathered relic from the past.

In a clever nod to their original function, sections of terra-cotta drain tile have been ingeniously stacked to create a trickling, fern-crowned fountain.

PAINTERLY POTS

One easy, low-cost way to dress up a patio or deck is to give plain clay or redwood containers your own custom paint job. To achieve the bright results you see here, all you need is latex paint, a brush, a sponge—and your own creative powers.

Before you begin, it's a good idea to waterproof your pot, so it will be both functional and long lasting. (Just be aware that waterproofing makes pots more moisture retentive, so you may need to adjust your watering accordingly.) First, coat the pot inside and out with water-based, nontoxic liquid waterproofing; it's available from well-stocked hardware stores. Let this dry for 24 hours. Then coat the interior with roofing compound or asphalt emul-

sion (look in garden centers or hardware stores), stopping 2 inches short of the pot rim.

Now comes the creative part. Using latex paint, you can create your own designs or copy the ones shown here. The southwestern motif was achieved by cutting out a triangular piece of sponge, applying paint to one side, and pressing it onto the pot. To paint a solid-colored pot like the purple one, just apply paint with a small roller. Or you can combine the two methods, as shown on the yellow pot with blue swirls: roll on a solid color, let it dry, and then add a design with brushes or sponges. For a final coordinating touch, you might coat the saucer with waterproofing; when it's dry, paint just its rim. Be sure that all pots are thoroughly dry before planting in them.

artful touches

Stroll across the checkerboard
"carpet" of this wild and
whimsical topiary bedroom to
the four-poster boxwood bed
with its canopy of grapevines.
Years of patient pruning and
training went into creating
this amusing garden "room."

It's pure fantasy! The
Seven Dwarfs preside
along the eaves of a
quaint garden dovecote
(above), surrounded
by a technicolor
perennial bed.

In an outdoor dining
room with a difference,
the table at right is
"set" with a fragrant
tablecloth of woolly
thyme. Above it arch
wisteria and glass
Victorian nightlights, to
make a bower of delicate
hue and heady scent.

If you like playful nostalgia in your garden, try staging a vignette around an antique claw-foot bathtub (left), or fill crockery (below) with succulents or similarly diminutive plants.

Below, an antique lantern hung on one post of a rose-covered pergola lends a sense of old-time graciousness to this garden.

This garden corner brims with country charm since the addition of an antique galvanized tub filled with geraniums and lobelia. A classic old watering can stands at the ready for sprinkling the planted bouquet.

artful touches

contemporary
treasures

CONTEMPORARY ART CREATED ESPECIALLY FOR THE GARDEN has a freedom of spirit that makes it a joy to look at. These pieces are as individual as their creators—and can play a variety of roles in a range of garden styles and situations. Often, modern garden artwork is on a monumental scale that would make it impossible to display indoors. In an expansive garden, a very large sculpture makes a bold yet appropriate statement. And in the smaller spaces within which most of us live, the colors and forms of contemporary art pieces can have a remarkably strong visual impact on the viewer. Sometimes a sculpture "garden" is the perfect design solution for a city lot or a space where shade or hardscape makes it difficult to plant anything. In other gardens, it's the interplay between plants and art that makes it all work.

Seated on a stretch of emerald lawn, the dark forms of two bronze female figures are an arresting focal point.

If you're designing a garden land-scape from scratch, you may be seeking the perfect focal piece for an important view. On the other hand, if you're a collector wanting a natural setting for a work by your favorite sculptor, or a first-time buyer who's just been captivated by a piece at a garden gallery, acquiring the artwork may come first. In that case, your challenge is to find just the right spot for it. (If you've bought a large, heavy piece, select your spot carefully—you won't want to move it later!)

When choosing contemporary artwork for the garden, you can't go far wrong if you simply buy what you love. That may be anything from an abstract steel sculpture with clean, bold lines to a ceramic nude, or from a delicate wire arch to a massive granite fountain. Either way, there's an excitement about choosing and siting original works of art in your own garden. And once they're in place, they will provide years of delight and satisfaction every time you look at them. Let the works shown on these pages be starting points for your own collection.

The sensuous folded form of a fountain molded of concrete shows dramatically against a spare back-drop of wall and tree trunks.

This unusual garden wall is fashioned in gleaming stainless steel to create a stunning picture of reflected light and subtle color. The "gallery" features photos of plants printed on sheets of steel using a special emulsion process.

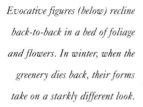

Birds of every feather have long fascinated creators of both folk and fine art. At left, a handcrafted bird struts on pitchfork "legs"; the elegant bird of prey at right perches on a base of rough natural stone.

Evocative figures (below) recline back-to-back in a bed of foliage and flowers. In winter, when the greenery dies back, their forms take on a starkly different look.

A masterpiece by a noted British sculptor needs no more display than a simple pedestal, with the light touch of blooming Japanese anemones for foreground.

Gleaming amid the foliage—both real and fabricated (in the case of the ivy)—the dark form of a cast-metal bird comes as a subtle surprise.

The bold presence of Back Flip—a large-scale piece sculpted in rusted metal—transforms this simple meadow garden into a contemporary art gallery.

A monumental "wave," fittingly encrusted with shells, curls above a living "shore" of colorful perennial flowers.

Below, a bronze lioness raises her head from feather grasses to evoke the African savannah in a domestic landscape.

artful touches

Leaves, intricate creations of art and nature, complement one another on a garden wall. The molded-concrete specimen on the left was cast from a huge natural leaf of the rice paper plant and then cleverly painted. An abutilon blooms to its right.

A gazing ball gleams in the center of an abstract "morning glory" set atop a tall pedestal.

In true southwestern spirit, this one-of-a-kind cactus was fashioned in metal and painted in the bold colors of its region; more examples of this artist's exuberant work appear in the background.

Rainbow-colored blown-glass flowers bloom on twining metal stems in this artist's garden. The interplay of living flowers with handcrafted ones gives the tableau added interest.

Silhouetted against a stucco wall, an original work in metal contributes a slender vertical accent.

Set into a vibrantly colored stucco wall, the sinuous curve of a fiber-optic light sculpture is an arresting vision by day or night.

artful touches

the art
of illusion

IN **A SMALL GARDEN,** you can use a few imaginative tricks
with mirrors, windows, and paint to expand space and multiply images. A
mirror at the end of a series of overarching trees or a window set into a wall
can create the illusion of a much larger garden. Even fragments of old mirrors
propped among plants against a fence can reflect light and images in surprising
and appealing ways. (Just be sure that sharp edges won't harm children or
pets.) And if you face a blank garage wall or have a tiny patio that ends abrupt-
ly at the property line, you can work wonders with a painted *trompe l'oeil*
scene—anything from a jungle paradise to a faux gate that appears to lead into

another part of the
garden. Even in larger
spaces, a well-placed
mirror can add drama
and surprise when set
behind a statue or
placed at the end of
a walkway. On these
pages you'll find
plenty of ideas for
artful illusions that
you can conjure up
in your own garden.

Like a tunnel into
another dimension, a
hypnotic allée of
golden bamboo (right)
ends in a mirror—
and thus extends
into infinity.

Where does illusion
end and reality begin?
Potted ferns and
shrubs, as well as slen-
der twigs and branches
dangling from above,
blend with the delicate
leafy traceries of a
botanical mural.

The lavender fields of Provence seem to stretch out beyond a stone-framed opening in a patio wall; skillful trompe l'oeil painting created this charming illusion to open up a small, Mediterranean-inspired space.

How many pots are there? A cleverly placed mirror doubles the number, adding depth and encouraging the viewer to take a second look. The pot planted with geraniums is a piquant contrast to its three empty siblings.

When you first encounter them, these ladies and their dog may give you a start, as if you have suddenly wandered into the 19th century! Their genteel presence focuses this small garden of greenery; a nearby gazebo (shown on pages 32–33) contributes to the delightful illusion.

Reflections—realistic, distorted, or imagined— have been used to artistic purpose at least since medieval times. Two clever contemporary spins for the garden are shown here. Below, a curved mirror miniaturizes a statue across the way. At right, a simple setup teases the viewer with the question, Mirror or frame?

artful touches

classic
ornaments

FROM THE CLAY POTS AND JARS of ancient peoples and
the statuary of the Greeks and Romans to the potted palms and tea pavilions of the Victorian era, "classic" models for garden ornaments have
been handed down to us for centuries. In the grand gardens of
Italian Renaissance princes, myriad fountains kept company with statues representing the gods, goddesses, and mythical creatures of
antiquity. These features retained their popularity through the 17th
and 18th centuries, when they appeared in the vast formal gardens
of the French nobility. In the 19th century, with the rise of the
middle classes, reproductions of classical-era statues and fountains
in cast stone and iron elbowed one another in many a smaller
garden.

*Clematis tendrils
weave old-fashioned
charm through
a Victorian-style
curlicue gate.*

Today, Victorian garden relics are prized antiques, and most ear-
lier ornaments are strictly museum pieces. Although "the real thing"
from times past is available to only a
lucky few, handsome reproductions now
abound. Statuary, fountains, urns, even
pillars and pedestals cast in stone, cement,
metals, and newer synthetic materials are
widely sold in garden shops and galleries.
Sundials of every description are also
available. Many of these new pieces look
almost as authentic as their vintage
ancestors, especially when they've
weathered a little and acquired patches of
moss or lichen (see page 49).

You'll see a wide selection of artifacts
in the classical style on the next few pages;
notice how attractive they look in conjunc-
tion with carefully chosen, complementary
plantings.

*Decorative birdbaths
like the one shown
above were an
inspired late-19th-
century addition to the
garden. The softly
weathered and mossy
lady at right exempli-
fies the type of statue
that has been a staple
of garden decor for
centuries.*

artful touches

CARING FOR YOUR TREASURES

Ornaments made especially for gardens are meant to remain outdoors in all weather; in fact, many look even better when nature has aged them. Still, the following measures will ensure that your treasures will survive the seasons—especially freezing winters—in good shape.

When you buy a work of art or an antique in a shop, ask how to care for it. Generally, objects fashioned of untreated iron and some kinds of steel will rust if not protected. Iron will eventually rust through; most steel will rust to a certain point and then stop. You may want to let iron pieces rust naturally for a while before sealing them (see page 10). Contemporary sculptures made of steel may have a baked-on coating to inhibit rust. But it's a good idea to apply a 50-50 mix of turpentine and linseed oil to most other steel semiannually.

Bronze, new or old, benefits from a yearly coating of wax—either one formulated for treating artworks or a simple car wax. However, over time unwaxed bronze develops the streaks and verdigris that you see on public statues—you may find that more attractive.

Stone, cast stone, and cast concrete ornaments are best left alone. If granite or marble develops stains, you can clean it with a weak bleach solution (1 part bleach to 10 parts water).

In cold-winter climates, pots and urns can crack if water or wet soil in them freezes and expands. It's best not to plant directly in a large, heavy container; instead, fit a plastic pot inside it that can be moved in for the winter. If you do plant directly, empty the pot before winter freezes, and keep its interior dry. If you must leave it filled, moderate expansion by lining it with plastic foam peanuts before adding potting soil, or by sinking a 2-inch-wide shaft of plastic foam through the soil's center.

Wood weathers and breaks down quickly. Strictly ornamental pieces may look best if left to weather, but you can coat these, as well as functional pieces like furniture, with a clear wood preservative.

Every culture has its classic statuary. Above, a traditional Thai representation of the Buddha presides in contemplative calm over a lush, tropical-looking pond; below, a Grecian-style bust elevated on a pedestal brings elegant formality to a small garden niche.

Long before clocks, sundials marked the hours. Armillary spheres (above) are formed of rings bisected by an arrow indicating the angle of the earth's axis. The arrow's shadow moves around hourly marks shown on the primary ring. The simplest sundial—the familiar horizontal type (below)—has a triangular gnomon for casting a shadow on hours ticked off on the base.

This antique marble wall fountain has the graceful lines of a classical fixture.

The pineapple form of this finial is an old emblem of welcome and hospitality.

This faithful stone dog has sat waiting under its tree for many years, welcoming visitors with an offering of fruit in a stone basket.

The lady has no head! A lighthearted twist on a classical "ruin" is achieved by imaginative planting.

At left, a graceful maiden bearing an urnful of foliage enhances the illusion created by the false-perspective latticework trellis behind her. Together they create the impression of a three-dimensional garden "room."

A slender terra-cotta urn is embellished with the elaborate reliefs, or raised patterns, associated with traditional Tuscan pottery.

Reminiscent of the resting places provided for strolling visitors in the vast landscape gardens of Europe, the sheltered stone seat at left boasts an eye-catching medallion wrought of rusted metal.

In a setting that recalls the many-columned courtyards of ancient gardens, a bronze mask spouts fresh water into a pool dotted with aquatic plants.

The Victorians excelled at creating ornate gazebos that served as garden focal points as well as charming spots for tea or a chat. The modern example at left replicates their style.

ornamental pots

ALTHOUGH WE OFTEN PAY MORE ATTENTION TO THE PLANT it contains than to the pot itself, a beautiful or unique container can make a style statement on its own. A grand, ornate stone or cast-iron urn, for example, may be raised on a pedestal or positioned as a dramatic focal point at the end of a long walkway, to be viewed from afar.

A single tall oil jar may be laid on its side among grasses and other plants, or you might arrange a collection of pots in mixed sizes and materials. On the other hand, imaginative pairings of plant colors and forms with spectacular or unusual containers is an art form in itself, and one that you can refine and perfect from year to year.

Be sure to recognize that, of all the objects you display in your garden, containers can be the most vulnerable to winter's assaults because of the contraction and expansion that cause cracks and worse. Care for your prized containers accordingly; see page 30 for guidance.

As with any kind of artwork, seek out and acquire what you love. Whether it's an antique urn or trough, or a brand-new pot painted in extravagant colors, it will find its place in your garden as a quintessential expression of your personality and style. The containers shown on these pages are just a small sample of the treasures you can discover for your own garden.

Purposely tilted containers show off a profusion of hydrangeas, licorice plant, and petunias.

Pairing an empty glazed urn with variegated canna leaves (above) makes the most of sunlight's transformational effects.

Looking like the casually littered site of an archeological excavation, the arrangement of urns and foxgloves opposite is actually a carefully composed tableau.

The extensive gardens associated with stately homes often feature large, fine old stone urns displayed on pedestals; the one shown above looks particularly lovely bathed in late-afternoon sun, in concert with blooming lavender. Below, a collection of terra-cotta pots, each brimming with annuals and hung on a fence, conveys a completely different mood with its mixed colors, textural variety, and asymmetry.

Planted containers in traditional styles are wonderful enhancements to many gardens. At top, a stone urn of classic form bestows grandeur on humble hen and chicks. Below it, a country-style "wicker" basket overflows with roses and pansies.

Nestled in a late-spring border, the elegant form of a large glazed jar provides a strong focus for one corner of this closely planted garden.

A classic Tuscan terra-cotta trough gains importance from its eminence atop a wall; papyrus planted in the foreground softens the look.

A generous helping of artistic imagination went into the creation of this unique pot-and-plant composition. Note that the succulents in the pots echo those growing at ground level.

You can create a delightful vignette simply by painting terra-cotta pots to color-coordinate them with your chosen plantings. Here, the pot design harmonizes with bright pink asters (in the pot) and flowering sedums (around it).

art from nature

the magic
of water

ALMOST ANY GARDEN CAN GAIN DIMENSION FROM WATER, that most changeable of elements. Captured and directed through lively fountains and small streams, it imparts both light and music to the garden. Gathered into quiet ponds, it nurtures plant and bird life and also provides a mirror to contain lovely reflected images. Water brings coolness and serenity to the garden and masks outside noises with its trickling and splashing. It's no wonder that water was a main element in the ancient gardens of Rome and Persia, as well as in the later traditional gardens and landscapes of Europe and Asia. Cascades, pools, and fountains were principal features in Renaissance Italian gardens, just as pools and canals were central to the great gardens of France and England. In Chinese and Japanese gardens, microcosmic bodies of water imitated the natural world by representing oceans, lakes, and rivers on a small scale.

When you introduce water into a garden you take advantage of not only its own inherent beauty and appeal, but also the charm of structures like fountains and pools that you use to contain and direct it. For example, a pool and fountain made of colorful tiles is highly decorative; the sunlight playing on the falling water adds yet another dimension of pleasure to the sight. You may design a formal garden around such a fountain and pool, or you may choose a less dominant water feature that looks as if nature left it there by happy accident. Even a small basin with a simple spout of water trickling into it can conjure up a primeval oasis.

You can devise a water feature for any garden, no matter what its style. From a humble tub of water containing aquatic plants to a waterfall tumbling over rocks, from a formal fountain to a naturalistic pond, water elements are as versatile as they are effective. On the next few pages, you'll find plenty of inspiration for ways to add water's beauty to your garden.

In the cool, fern-lined grotto shown below, a miniature waterfall spills from an earthenware jug set into a wall of rock.

A graceful dancer's sculpted figure draws the viewer's eye irresistibly to this enchanting garden pond.

At right, silvery water mirrors the sky in a spectacular series of pools linked by small canals. This elegant composition, which recalls the water channels featured in classic gardens of the past, offers a gleaming vista as it stretches away between rows of clipped yews.

*Falling water adds
soothing music to
the garden. You can
create a waterfall
that imitates nature
(above left) or, on
a more modest scale,
a quiet trickle such
as that produced by
a Japanese-inspired
tsukubai arrangement
(above right).*

*Pouring into a wide,
gleaming bowl, a
stream of silvered
water complements the
gray, misty landscape
around it. The sleek,
contemporary form
and muted metallic hue
of the fountain also
harmonize with the
forms and colors of the
surrounding palms
and lavender.*

Subtlety and a touch of mystery are the hallmarks of this understated composition in stone and moss. Water drips from the time-weathered wall fountain and meanders along a zigzag path created by widened joints between the paving stones.

Art and nature merge in the lifelike fountain above, which was cast in color-washed concrete from a gunnera-leaf mold. The leaf unfurls over an iris-edged pond, a cool trickle of water spilling gently from its delicately detailed edges.

Beckoning from the endpoint of a path edged with a profusion of flowering plants, a moss-patterned fountain invites visitors to further explore this garden's delights.

Thoroughly at home in its garden pond, a stone frog (above) spouts forth a stream of water. In a more formal spirit (right), a classic multitiered fountain looks equally fitting in a bed of lush bergenia. The interplay of sunlight and water lends this composition an enchanting beauty.

Perfect serenity reigns in this timeless scene. The still water reflects the image of an arched Chinese camelback bridge. Built on a grand scale, it's high enough to allow small boats to pass under its graceful span.

As in nature, a hollow in a rock captures a tiny pool of water to create a birdbath— here, for a petite cast-metal bird.

The elegant spa below doubles as a reflecting pool. The symmetrical design, featuring twin arbors, is formal in feeling yet softened by the lush greenery growing around and overhead.

Coming upon these sculptures (above) in the midst of a forest garden is like dis- covering lost ruins. Intriguing metal spires mist the air; one spills water into a basin beneath it. At left, a color-washed concrete pool nestled amid low-growing plantings bears along a flotilla of tiny water lilies and a single glass bauble.

art from nature

sculpting
the elements

B ASIC ELEMENTS OF THE NATURAL WORLD—rock, wood, and plants—can be an important part of your garden decor. You may use their native forms as sculpture, calling attention to their beauty by positioning them where they will be noticed and appreciated. You may also shape them or combine them with other elements to create original structures that become works of art.

Rocks, the foundation of the garden, reveal their subtle colors and textures as well as their strong forms when placed amid plantings or reconceived as seats, walkways, or columns. Similarly, a gnarled piece of wood can look like a sculpture, especially if mounted on a base or wall or skillfully arranged with other elements. With minimal reshaping, a substantial piece of wood can become a wonderfully individualistic garden seat or table (see page 38). Living plants themselves, chosen for their specific natural forms and colors, can be installed as dramatic accents in the garden. They can also be trained into living sculptures—in the fantastic shapes of topiary, in espaliered patterns on walls and trellises, and as living arbors or tunnels interwoven overhead. Finally, don't overlook the power of light and shadow to shape and enhance your garden composition. Bare wintry tree branches that cast a dramatic shadow on a white wall, trellises that filter sunlight into an intricate pattern cast on the lawn below—these visual effects can be every bit as decorative as a solid piece of sculpture. For imaginative examples of artistry employing nature's elements, look no further than these pages.

When you really examine a boulder, you become aware of the subtleties of its color, texture, and form. Rock varies greatly from region to region; shown below are (left to right) desert cloud, desert paint, imagination stone, and holey fieldstone.

Above, a lichen-spotted monolith placed in a clearing evokes the venerated standing stones of old. At right, the torchlike shapes of euphorbia make a lively backdrop for mounds of neatly clipped lavender.

Tracing a nautilus's contours, the spiral of stones
below transforms a patio corner into a work of art.
You might use specially selected river stones or found
rocks to create your own design—then alter or
rearrange it as inspiration calls.

Set in a sea of white sand, the carefully placed stones above
compose a picture of serenity in a Japanese "dry" garden.
In this tradition, rocks may symbolize mountains and
islands or simply form an abstract composition. Below, two
handsome boulders are set off by vertical accents of flowers
and grasses. Both plants and rocks look as if they have
always been here, despite having been placed by clever hands.

A benchmark in the wilderness, this lone rock rests
atop a mossy mound encircled by pine needles. Artful
placement gives it the status of sculpture in its
woodland clearing.

At left, moss softens the shoulder of a massive boulder. Wine-colored Japanese maple, rhodo-dendrons, and ferns grow closely around its base. Above, a sprinkling of azalea blossoms suggests an offering of brilliant color atop a dark stone altar.

QUICK "ANTIQUING" WITH MOSS

Nothing gives a garden that long-established look like velvety green moss spreading over rocks and statuary in lovely irregular patterns. But what if your magnificent boulder or cast-stone statue was set down in your garden, new and pristine, just last week? Do you have to wait years for it to acquire that softened, time-worn look?

Luckily, no. You can actually speed up the growth of moss in shady areas by painting garden objects such as cement or cast-stone statues and porous rocks with the following formula. First, dissolve a fist-size lump of porcelain clay (available at craft shops or ceramic supply companies) in about 3 cups of water or until the mixture has the consistency of a thick milkshake. Then combine the clay suspension with 1 cup of undiluted liquid fish fertilizer and 1 cup of moss gathered from sidewalk cracks or from a moist spot in your own garden. Thoroughly whip the mixture in an old blender or with a wire whisk, then paint it on your rock or statuary with a brush. As you paint, try to imitate the natural patchy growth patterns of moss: the way it grows more thickly in crevices and along northern sides. In a moist, shady location, you may perceive a soft layer of moss within several months. (Misting the piece may aid its development.)

Fallen blossoms spangle an old stone trough and wall fountain with their pink petals, lending a delicate springtime touch to the rough-hewn stone.

For centuries, roughly shaped staddle stones were used by British farmers to raise their granaries off the ground. This venerable old example rests in comfortable retirement amid lamb's ears, grasses, and sage.

At near right, rock and driftwood lie inter-mingled as if deposited by a rushing stream. Actually, this composi-tion was shaped by human hands and then left to settle naturally into the landscape. At far right, a care-fully composed granite altar for birds offers a tiny pool of water brightened by a sprinkling of petals.

This unique garden installation relies on a combination of shaped "stone" and grass for its simple yet powerful effect. Concrete spheres are set on concentric circles mowed into a lush green lawn. The chair frame and mirror add a touch of surreal intrigue to the composition.

The naturally spherical form of the barrel cactus is appealing and dramatic—especially when many plants are clustered closely, as in this desert courtyard. The window in the background mirrors the round shapes, and the ocotillos provide a spiky counterpoint.

In a study in contrasts, formal, deep green boxwood hedges restrain exuberant chartreuse barberries to form a colorful geometric pattern. A cast-stone pineapple finial marks the axis point.

*Certain pieces of
driftwood and old,
gnarled tree trunks are
natural sculptures.
With imaginative
placement and a few
minor alterations,
someone has made us
visualize the crocodile
in the old log at right.
Below it, combining a
gnarled cedar stump
with brilliant
rhododendrons and
azaleas in bloom
results in a natural-
looking still life that
illuminates its wood-
land setting.*

*Many a gardener
delights in painting
pictures with flowers.
Above, the contrast
of brilliant yellow aloe
blossoms against an
intensely purple wall
makes a vibrant
composition worthy
of Gauguin.*

*Some plants' forms
are so striking as to
qualify them as
works of art. This
New Zealand flax's
fountain of leaves rises
regally from its bed of
grasses; a well-placed
earthenware urn
provides a focal point
and pulls together the
whole mise-en-scène.*

Many seasons went into the sculpting of this mighty oak. Its natural growth pattern, in partnership with patient training, has created an awesome sculpture of massive, serpentine limbs.

With time and patience, you can create a natural sculpture garden with topiary, the art of pruning and training shrubs and trees into ornamental shapes. Below, a host of simply shaped English yews is lit by a wash of golden sunlight.

Above, this topiary feline peering over the hedge is sure to surprise and delight passersby. Topiary gardens on the great estates of Europe often feature such fanciful creatures sculpted in shrubbery.

art from nature

EASY ESPALIER

Perfected by 16th- and 17th-century European gardeners, the technique of espalier—training trees or vines to grow in a flat, patterned framework against a wall—has two ornamental purposes. It saves space in small gardens, and it adds an intriguing decorative element of pattern, light, and shadow to any wall or fence.

You can espalier a vine or shrub using materials as simple as wire and eyescrews. A diamond pattern like that shown here is a strong, straightforward design that will work almost anywhere.

Into wood fences or walls, attach eyescrews threaded with 12- to 14-gauge galvanized wire. Space the wires about 18 inches apart. Plastic clothesline also makes a strong, inconspicuous framework; attach it to fence or siding as you would wire, using eyescrews.

In the photo above, the supporting grid is made of tubular iron. If you want to use a ready-made framework of pipe or wood lattice, fasten it to a wood wall using lag screws, galvanized nails, or U-shaped staples. Use wood spacer blocks or metal washers to create "breathing" space between trellis and wall. If the wall is of masonry, choose screws, lag screws, or threaded rods with a nut and washer, all driven into expanding anchors.

It may take several years for the full design to become clear. Keep pruning off branches that obscure the pattern, and you'll be rewarded with a handsome vertical display. In our example, star jasmine is used. Other perennial vines to try are ivies, some cotoneasters, and vine maple (*Acer circinatum*). Check nurseries in your area for other suitable plants that can be readily trained.

Light and shadow can be manipulated to create breathtaking effects. Below, beneath a graceful pergola supporting carefully trained apple trees, sunlight and shade cast lovely chiaroscuro patterns on the lawn.

In a perfect marriage of plants and structures, gauzy veils of wisteria cascade from the rafters of an arbor. The delicate texture and color of the dangling floral clusters contrast with the dark wood of the arbor to create a magical retreat.

In the clear southwestern desert air, light and darkness play out high drama against an intensely colored wall. This design takes advantage of the effects of shadow to create a large-scale optical illusion.

At right, the graceful curves of this gate and the arched trellis above it frame a lovely garden portrait beyond. The relative darkness on one side of the gate accentuates the brightness and color of the more distant view.

A wood lath trellis demonstrates the alchemy of light and shadow through the hours and seasons. In spring (top), bright sunlight traces its intricate patterns, along with the tree's shadow, in sharp lines on the grass. In winter (bottom), the quality of light changes, and the shadows are softened as they stretch across the white snow.

art from nature

birds in the garden

T HE PRESENCE OF BIRDS—the flash of a wing in the sunlight or a sweet, trilling song echoing in the still evening—adds an extra dimension of pleasure to our time spent in the garden. And the accessories we provide for them in the form of baths, houses, and feeders often have a charm all their own. Although strictly utilitarian structures are no doubt fine from the birds' point of view, a whimsical approach to their design and decoration is more fun for human observers. On these pages, ideas abound for fresh interpretations, from straw houses to baths that resemble sculpture. Do keep in mind, though, that some charming birdhouses are less than practical. They should have a section that opens to allow for annual cleaning. And any perch should be removed (some birds will sit on it and heckle the occupants!). Finally, place houses on metal poles or hang them from trees, well out of reach of cats and raccoons.

Amid a sea of lush plantings, wild birds can join their sculpted counterparts at the elegant concrete bird feeder below.

The log-cabin-in-the-meadow shown above is strictly for the birds. In contrast, the charming bird haven at right has also provided a home for plants: pansies, succulents, and ivy engulf its shingled roof and open porch.

artful
dividers

FENCES AND WALLS, and the gates that open through them, shape and define garden rooms as well as providing shelter, privacy, and an intimate sense of enclosure. They've been used to define outdoor space for centuries: think of the drystone walls that divide many a rural pasture, the enclosed gardens of medieval Europe, or the adobe-encircled mission gardens of Old California. Today, walls and fences help us define our own little garden corners in an ever-more-crowded world. At the same time they can be decorative features in themselves, as the examples on these pages clearly show.

Certain dividers are classic choices for particular settings: a white picket fence belongs to a New England cottage, whereas a simple, stark stucco wall will often complement a contemporary home. Usually walls are strong and sturdy—constructed of stone, concrete, brick, stucco, or adobe. They may look natural and rough-hewn or formal and smoothly textured. Their colors differ, too: materials like stone and adobe have naturally soft earth tones, whereas stucco or concrete may be colored in bold and surprising hues. Garden fences and screens may be solid or more open. Those made of wood are seen in a wide variety of colors and designs, from rustic board fencing to airy white latticework to Asian-inspired detailing. And that classic, the wrought-iron fence, is a perennial favorite.

With gates, the sky's the limit when it comes to material and design; in fact, on these pages you'll see one-of-a-kind gates that are real works of art. Many of the walls, fences, and gates shown here blend into a garden's design, but some are outstanding decorative elements in their own right.

A rustic branch fence is the perfect choice for enclosing this casual country garden; the intricate design of its panels raises it above mere utility.

Wrought iron can be simple or elaborate. At top, it's forged into a grapevine motif; below that, it accommodates recycled glass panels.

At right, dignity and grandeur characterize these meticulously crafted gateways. They usher visitors by stages into the wilder garden beyond.

The vine pattern on this distinctive handcrafted copper gate echoes the style of the vine-wreathed garden around it. Dressed with verdigris flourishes, the gate is topped off with a crosshatched trellis.

Set into an adobe wall, the carved wood portal above is a handsome example of traditional southwestern crafts.

The outdoor "room" shown below is loosely defined by "walls" of roses clambering over a graceful concrete-columned arbor washed in soft blue paint.

This wall of brick acts as a canvas for one artist's marvelously abstract "painting" in mosaic. Its features include swirls of color and pattern as well as built-in planters.

At left: two gardens, two gates, two equally delightful styles. A blue door-in the-wall gate (top), flanked by antique stone urns and smothered in roses, is a cottage-garden dream come true. Below it, a unique gate conceived from an assortment of metallic found objects and screening hints at the witty and imaginative spirit that reigns in the garden beyond.

At right: low walls that embrace raised planting or pool areas can be striking design elements in themselves. Free-form bas-relief tiles (top) sculpted in swirling shapes adorn the curved walls of a pool. A boldly painted and textured planter wall (center) zigzags along one side of a patio. Handmade tiles of intense lapis blue (bottom) crown the simple wood wall of a raised flower bed.

Curlicues adorn this charming wrought-iron fence worthy of a Victorian estate. Plantings—old-fashioned pansies and a backdrop hedge of boxwood—complement the traditional design and spirit of the fence.

What could make a more perfect backdrop for a cottage-garden flower border than a white picket fence? In the example below, a slight curve to the picket tops adds grace.

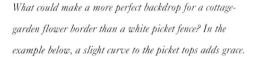

In the contemporary patio garden shown here, a living "fence" of horsetail creates a lush screen of greenery between two seating areas. Planting it between two paved areas keeps this enthusiastic spreader in check.

Walls, screens, and fences built of natural materials can be substantial in feeling or light and airy. A masterpiece of mixed masonry, a gatepost (top) is created from old brick, cut stone, and natural rock. The lightweight screen of woven bamboo shown beneath it, designed for a traditional Asian garden, affords privacy yet lets breezes through.

GARDEN GALLERIES

Like the walls in your home, your garden walls and fences can be wonderful display spaces for favorite art pieces. Of course, you can't hang your oil paintings outdoors. But works of art made from durable materials such as ceramic, wood, and some metals can add distinction and color to your garden walls (see page 22, top left). Decorative folk art pieces and collectibles can also look terrific, especially on informal wood fences and screens. Try hanging up a bright hand-painted birdhouse, an antique sign, a faux-antique plaque, or a sturdily crafted ceramic plate. Or display your own found objects—for example, a sculptural piece of driftwood or a selection of old-time gardening tools.

Sometimes a large or bold piece will look best as the only object on a wall. In other situations, a grouping of small related items is effective and quite charming. Often an art piece on a wall can be enhanced by "framing" it with living vines, so long as the foliage is kept well trimmed (see page 81, bottom right).

When you match art to a wall or fence, keep weight in mind. A wood fence may not be sturdy enough to support a heavy ceramic piece, for example.

If your chosen piece doesn't come ready to hang, you can usually attach an eye screw or hanging clip to its back. Then hang it on a nail or nails driven into a wood wall or fence—or, for a masonry wall, on a screw or lag screw driven into an expanding anchor.

beautiful basics

decoration
underfoot

THE PAVINGS, PATIOS, AND DECKS OF A GARDEN
are the "floors" of your outdoor room; paths and steps are like the
halls and stairways. The materials you select to create these
surfaces and passageways make an important
design statement in your garden. For instance, an
arrangement of irregular stepping-stones dotted
with moss or plants such as creeping thyme and
chamomile looks soft and natural, whereas a patio of
pavers interlaid with handmade tiles in rainbow colors looks
highly decorative and individualistic.

*Square paving stones
set corner-to-corner
make an appealing
diamond-patterned
path beneath a rustic
hazelwood arch.*

The scope for creativity is wide. Underfoot surfaces can
be intricately arranged mosaics or sleek wood decking laid in
interesting patterns, informal arrangements of stone and
gravel or precise geometric layouts of mortared brick. A beautifully designed and crafted path, patio, or set of steps can be
either quietly decora-
tive, carrying out an
overall theme in color
and materials, or an
eye-catching
surprise—something
to notice and comment on.

Paths over water, such as small
bridges or elevated stepping-stones,
can be particularly delightful. These
pages offer an array of imaginative
approaches to creating unique and
beautiful surfaces underfoot in many
kinds of gardens, large and small.

*Natural materials,
artfully arranged,
make the garden
underfoot a delight to
traverse. An edging of
terra-cotta roofing tiles
(above) creates a sinu-
ous line between a bed
of Irish moss and a
swath of river stones.
At right, an imagina-
tive assortment of
subtly hued stones and
pebbles makes up a
natural mosaic of
stone and moss.*

A mosaic sunburst created with pebbles is the centerpiece of the lighthearted composition below; the high-backed wood chair guarded by boxwood standards in pots looks like a fantasy throne atop a regal dais.

Plants and pavings can work together in fascinating ways. At top, a checkerboard of pavers and planted squares neatly organizes the space. Below it, a path of railroad ties interspersed with gravel and mosses has a casual, naturalistic look.

Arranged in rays around a large, ornate ceramic jar, alternating strips of grass and concrete paving define this circular garden "room." Pairing a weathered Victorian ironwork bench with a rustic twig arbor completes this eclectic blend of textures and styles.

Peer among the myriad ferns, hostas, and maples in pots below, and you'll spy a delightful little hidden retreat. To reach it, you cross a simple granite-slab bridge over a pond with a fascinating whirlpool effect.

Paths across water have special appeal. Tall octagonal stepping-stones (top) lead across still water; a more substantial bridge of moss-edged pavers fords a spillway (center). At bottom, a handsome "bridge" of boulders and wood platforms zigzags past lovely reflections.

Brick paving takes on new pizzazz (left) when laid in a crazy-quilt pattern—an appropriate complement to a relaxed setting like this one. A geometric pattern (above) of bricks and gravel is more formal in style.

Path design can take many directions. Clockwise from top left: an understated brick path separates frothy lavender borders; a handsome mixture of brick, stone, and dark gravel ends in a circle; recycled manhole covers forge an urban trail through suburban grasses; the North Wind doth blow across an intricate mosaic composition; mysterious stone faces smile up from a colorful bed of gravel and plantings; a subtle repeating design etched in concrete leads the eye to this path's end.

Bright blue ceramic tiles set amid bricks pick up this garden's blue-and-terra-cotta color scheme, evident in the hand-thrown ceramic pot and in the flowers' hues.

PERSONALIZED PAVERS

A path of handmade mosaic pavers created from pieces of tile or pottery can add special charm and a very personal touch to your garden, especially if the pieces have fond associations for you. Perhaps you've broken a favorite dish or pottery piece, or maybe you have colorful tiles left over from a remodeling project. By recycling them, you can create a little pathway of several pavers or use a single one as an accent.

For each stepping-stone you want to make, start with a ready-made concrete paver purchased at a building or garden center. (Also purchase grout and tile adhesive from a building center or tile store.) Keeping your design simple and using a limited palette of colors, loosely sketch it on the paver.

Protect your eyes with goggles and wear rubber gloves when working on this project. In a heavy-duty, zip-top plastic bag, seal up a whole tile or large pottery piece. With a hammer, gently break up the tile into pieces of an appropriate size. Repeat this with the other tiles.

Apply tile adhesive to the back of the pieces and place them on the paver, following your design. Make sure you allow sufficient space between pieces to apply grout, and let the layout dry for 1 hour.

In a small, disposable container, mix the tile grout to a thick consistency (follow the package directions). Wearing rubber gloves, press the grout evenly into the spaces between the pieces. The grout should be flush with the outer edge of the stone all around.

After the grout has dried for 10 minutes, wipe off any excess with a damp sponge, but don't remove too much grout. Shine the tile with a towel and let it dry for 24 hours. If you wish, you can then apply an outdoor sealer. Now you're ready to position your paver in the garden.

beautiful basics

accent on furnishings

EVERY OUTDOOR ROOM NEEDS FURNITURE if it's to beckon people to pause and look, relax and dream, or enjoy an alfresco meal. Furnishings may be as simple as a bench hewn from a log or stone, or as ornate as a Victorian confection of wire or cast iron. Like any other furniture, an outdoor grouping should be chosen for comfort and practicality as well as for good looks. At the same time, furnishing a garden seems to invite a more relaxed, playful attitude. You may feel freer to choose a unique piece that you can use strictly for its visual interest—as an art object or sculpture—to bring interesting colors and forms to the scene. Garden art galleries now feature handcrafted pieces that are literally works of art. You can also have fun shopping for old pieces, whether antiques or flea market finds. A piece of furniture that's a little too funky for indoors might be just the touch you need outside. (But be sure that, if you want to keep it for a while, it's reasonably weatherproof.) Often you can paint an old wood or metal piece to give it new life. And don't overlook the possibility of creating seats and tables out of things not necessarily intended for furniture—found pieces of rock or concrete, barrels, chimney flues—the only limit is your imagination.

Nestled in a colorful bed of lilies, marigolds, and foliage, a unique metal garden chair makes a stunning focal point.

The Victorian-style cast-iron bench on the facing page harmonizes perfectly with a potted white nicotiana and the licorice plant, ivy, and petunias gathered around its feet. Both the paint color and the old-fashioned design contribute to the charm of the scene.

Furniture that's manufactured for the garden may be crafted of wood, metal, stone, or synthetic materials. Wood can look handsome and sleek when carefully finished and maintained, or rustic and weathered when left to the elements. Painted wood has a charm all its own, and a bright yellow or red chair set out on an expanse of lawn can be a stunning outdoor accent. Rustic furniture of woven willow, poplar, or laurel twigs is another popular choice that can look just right in country or woodsy settings.

Metal garden furniture has been popular since Victorian days, when fancy designs in wirework and cast iron had their heyday. True antiques may have a patina of age in the form of rust or chipped paint; they can look charming this way, or you can restore or paint them (see page 10). Modern reproductions are often made of cast aluminum or steel, which is lighter and less expensive. And metal furniture in contemporary styling is a sleek and stylish choice.

A true garden furniture classic, in use for centuries, is the stone bench—in smoothly finished marble or rough-hewn stone. Such a piece will establish itself as a permanent and well-loved fixture in any garden.

This variation on the American Adirondack chair (above) has been painted a brilliant hue and surrounded by petunias and verbena, to make it an eye-catcher as well as a comfy place to sit. Another enticing retreat is the bower of willow shown below. Over and around the seat, which is woven of willow branches, is an enclosure created by pleaching together living willows.

The basic wood garden bench lends itself to an array of attractive design interpretations. The white-painted example shown at top is a one-of-a-kind contemporary design. The weathered Lutyens bench below it, now a classic, was designed by British architect Sir Edwin Lutyens around the turn of the century.

FIVE-MINUTE FLAGSTONE TABLE

A stylish garden table doesn't have to be expensive or compli-
cated to make. Here's one you can put together in a few minutes with materials from a building supply yard that specializes in
masonry. Our example's top is a single piece of hand-picked Arizona
flagstone about 21 inches wide by 32 inches long. The base is created from two 24-inch-tall chimney flue liners. (The liners in this
example are oval, but round or square ones are equally attractive.)
The terra-cotta liners are just the right height for a coffee table or
end table. Simply set the legs 6 to 8 inches apart on a firm, level
surface, center the flagstone over them.

*A fresh touch for the familiar twig chair is a coat of
paint. Here the designer has chosen a striking magenta
shade, which is echoed by the petunias planted alongside.*

*Natural materials are
formally shaped to
create this wonderful
stone-and-topiary
"sofa"; clipped
boxwood hedges form
the back, arms, and
skirt for a simple
stone bench.*

A river of oak flows around a living tree; the grooved surface, as well as the general outline, of this free-form bench suggests the rings in a cross section of a tree trunk.

A quartet of sophisticated wicker chairs painted an appealing shade of deep red (above right) creates an intimate gathering spot beneath mature shade trees in this attractive garden room. In a more playful spirit, the room shown below it features a friendly jumble of weathered furniture, including an antique sideboard and a mirror-paned "window."

Shining surfaces and simple forms characterize these contemporary furnishings. The metal rocking chair shown above gleams against its more traditional backdrop. The curvaceous metal-frame lounge chairs at right make perfect companions for the sleek, cylindrical metal planters.

A massive concrete dining table (below)
stands ready for large-scale outdoor
entertaining. Antique wirework chairs that
have been allowed to acquire a patina of
rust lighten the effect. Together, the pieces
bring complex personality to the patio.

In a carefully composed patio scene,
a handmade table holds center stage,
seconded by simple but elegant metal chairs.
The backdrop is a mirror framed by roses
and purple clematis.

inviting
retreats

W HETHER OPEN LIKE ARBORS AND GAZEBOS or enclosed like summerhouses, garden retreats are irresistibly inviting structures. They offer a perfect combination—the airiness and charm of the outdoors with the comfort and enclosure of an intimate room. When artfully integrated into the landscape, they can be great visual accents, too.

An arbor or pergola (a garden passageway comprising a series of arches) usually supports vines like wisteria, grape, or jasmine that clamber over it to form a living roof. The arbor itself may be of wood (painted or natural), twigs, or metal—plain or ornate. When well conceived, this combination of plants and structure makes a beautiful statement in almost any garden. A pergola can be particularly enticing when it frames a lovely view or has as its focal point an arresting object like a large urn or a statue placed at its far end.

Arbors may be partly attached to a house wall, but more substantial structures like gazebos, Japanese engawas, Southwest-style ramadas, and summerhouses are usually located some distance from the house. These provide focus to the landscape—either as a lovely vision seen across an expanse of lawn or water, or as a pleasant surprise encountered around a bend, tucked amid flowers and shrubbery. On the opposite end of the spectrum are garden retreats created entirely of living plants (see page 85, lower left).

On these pages, you'll see an inviting assortment of retreats, from leafy bowers to elegant gazebos—each one a beautiful enhancement to its garden surroundings.

The garden retreat below is a fantasy come true. Modeled on a traditional Indonesian platform house, this curtained "treehouse" is nearly engulfed in a colorful jungle of flowering plants and vines.

The latticed wood arbor at right gets an extra style boost from a coat of sky blue paint, picked up by the color of the wicker chair beside it. Arbor, chair, and foreground urn form a lovely still life amid the lush grasses and flowers.

*Arbors overgrown
with plants make
delightful hideaways.
Below, an ivy-covered
arbor frames a secret
walkway within its
graceful curves. The
wood-and-steel arch
shown beneath it is
loosely clad in flower-
ing vines that give it a
romantic feeling.*

*Reflected in still
waters, this lattice-
paneled gazebo sets off
both the pond at its feet
and the misty meadow
beyond. It's a lovely
focal point as well as
a tranquil resting spot.*

*A charming peaked-
roof garden shelter
offers quiet seclusion at
the end of a path
bordered by a fragrant
sea of shrub roses,
foliage, and grasses.*

Giving the impression of a classical ruin found among the trees, this graceful columned structure lends instant status to a pond bordered by lush greenery.

Visitors step across the stream on a path of stones to reach this idyllic rustic summerhouse, complete with gnarled-branch roof supports and a woven-twig chair by the front door.

Shelters can be formally stated or loosely implied elements in a garden setting. The airy Victorian ironwork gazebo shown at top is placed in a symmetrical arrangement of neatly trimmed shrubs. The retreat shown beneath it, in contrast, was created simply by planting overhanging trees and shrubs around a grass path to convey a sense of seclusion.

beautiful basics

the garden by night

ARTISTIC LIGHTING can make your garden
as remarkable at night as it is in the daytime,
often in a completely different way. Lighting can
be subtle or dramatic as well as merely pragmat-
ic. Carefully placed, it can shed a glow like that
of moonlight over the entire garden scene, or
focus dramatically on a single tree or shrub. Pools and
fountains, too, benefit from underwater or overhead illu-
mination. Such "staged" lighting is usually achieved with
concealed fixtures that are valued for the mood they create
rather than for their inherent good looks.

Other kinds of lights are made to be noticed; they're
beautiful works of art crafted in glass and metal or wood,
and are an effective part of the garden decor in the daytime.
These are a permanent part of the garden, attached to walls
or—distributed around the garden or along paths—wired
to transformers. Still another kind of lighting is temporary
and portable. This kind is
just plain fun; it includes
everything from south-
western luminarias (candles
set in bags of sand) to strings
of paper, metal, or other
small lanterns, to tabletop
glass-sided lanterns housing
candles, to lanterns or torch-
es on stakes lining paths and
walkways. For a selection of
wonderful ideas, turn the
page. (And for more on
garden lighting, see pages
108–109.)

*A garden light
"blooms" at the center
of a unique torch-style
fixture that's a real
work of art.*

*Lovely by day or night, a pear-shaped glass
light (above) glows atop a handsomely
designed post entwined with minilights and
clematis. In the lavishly staged night
garden shown at right, cleverly hidden light
fixtures flood wall fountains, plantings,
and sculptures with mystery.*

beautiful basics

This striking contemporary outdoor dining area gains thespian significance from recessed "footlights" uplighting two freestanding backdrop walls.

Simplicity is sometimes the best approach to garden lighting. At left, a colorful door is flanked by a pair of unobtrusive glass-and-metal lanterns that extend a bright welcome.

As evening falls, the rustic stone bench shown at right assumes a magical aura, thanks to the backlit many-paned window glowing behind it.

Fanciful lighting effects can bring a special touch to your night garden. Three comical water-spouting frogs (above) look extra lively when lit up; unusual pathway lights (right) resemble oversize bolts. Below, a stream lit from beneath flows over blue glass blocks and into a lighted pond.

SAND LANTERNS

To produce this elegant variation on luminaria candles set in sand, you use sand-filled flowerpots. Shop in nurseries for terra-cotta pots in decorative designs, or even for glazed or painted pots. Hurricane-lamp chimneys are available at home improvement stores and large import stores; you may also be lucky enough to find lovely older ones at flea markets. Here, the palette is soft and simple terra-cotta with white candles. But you can have fun playing with assorted shapes, sizes, and colors for both pots and candles. (Mix and match them for the liveliest look.)

To make a lamp, simply cover the inside of the pot's drain hole with a piece of masking tape or duct tape. Fill the pot with clean sand and insert the candle, pushing it deep enough to ensure stability. Then set in the chimney to give it a finished look and to protect the candle's flame from night breezes.

the art of design

a matter of style

CERTAIN KINDS OF ORNAMENTS *just naturally seem to belong in certain kinds of gardens. A white marble statue of Mercury is at home in a formal setting of parterres and reflecting ponds, but would look out of place in a split-rail-fence-enclosed meadow garden. On the other hand, a funky wooden chair that would look dowdy alongside clipped hedges and a marble fountain would blend right into an off-beat, casual setting. It's all a matter of style, as well as of personal taste. On these pages, we give you a quick tour of garden styles—past and present, formal and informal, foreign and homegrown.*

Traditional Japanese gardens are designed with great subtlety to look like "natural" landscapes. At right, this lovely adaptation of the style features a tsukubai fountain arrangement, carefully selected and sited boulders, and an artistically pruned maple tree.

What is garden style?

Style can be an elusive element to identify in a garden. One style may have its roots in a historical period, another in a particular region, and a third (as in the traditional Japanese garden) in a combination of the two. Often what gives a garden its character may be a mood rather than a time or place—free-spirited or nostalgic, relaxed or stately, playful or meditative.

The style and mood of a garden are expressed in a combination of hardscape (which includes walls, pavings, and other basics; see pages 62–89), plantings, furnishings, and decorative ornaments or accents. Far from being frosting on the cake, these last are—or should be—considered among the main contributions to the mix. As in any good recipe, all of the ingredients must work well together, balancing the basic flavors with the special touches that add spice.

The gracious garden at left features many elements of the classical style, including symmetrically placed stone urns, formally clipped shrubbery, and gravel walkways passing under an old stone arch. Below, this garden conveys old-fashioned comfort; the graceful fountain and wicker easy chair, as well as the rose garden, all bespeak the cozy Victorian era.

PERIOD STYLES have their origins in gardens popular during certain historical eras, such as the Italian Renaissance, the British Victorian era, or the American Colonial period. In this book, various formal European garden traditions from the past are loosely referred to by the term *classical,* for ease of reference. In general, these traditions share a formal approach, wherein art is imposed on nature to control and "tame" it. They feature symmetrical garden plans, water confined in clearly delineated pools and fountains, shrubbery and trees clipped and trimmed into neat geometric or representative shapes, and statuary modeled on classical Greek and Roman works (see pages 28–33). Often, architectural features such as columns and pediments echo those of ancient cultures, whether entire or "in ruins." Ornaments associated with these styles include classical statuary, fountains, stone benches, large urns, and sundials. Later variations on these themes were spun by the Victorians, who reproduced those same classical-era artifacts in cast iron. They added birdbaths, fancy benches and chairs, gazebos, and gazing globes to the pantheon of permanent garden ornaments.

tecture (including pottery, tile, and metalwork). A Mediterranean garden might feature a hardscape of stucco and local flagstone, large terra-cotta pots molded in centuries-old designs, splashing fountains, and native dry-climate plants like olive and oleander.

Although you may yearn for a garden in a regional style different from your own, any such re-creation will work best if there's some logical link to your climate. For example, a Mediterranean garden is easily reproduced in much of California, where the climate is comparable and supports similar plants and building materials; likewise, an English cottage garden will thrive in a lush, misty Pacific Northwest environment. And a Japanese-style garden is perfectly suited to a climate of greater extremes, to showcase the change of seasons so important to that tradition.

Above, a lovely West Coast interpretation of a Mediterranean garden features windmill palms, stucco walls, and an ornate stone urn. At right, a garden in upper New England embodies the romantic country style, complete with gazebo and graceful bridge.

REGIONAL STYLES have evolved over time in response to the climate, indigenous resources, and culture of a particular locale. Because every garden exists in a specific region, the decor of the garden often carries out the "themes" and aesthetic dictated by that area. Regional gardens reflect a combination of the plants native to that particular area and various cultural traditions, such as local architecture, available building materials, and the population's artisanal skills. For example, a southwestern garden would contain cacti and other desert plants, local construction materials such as adobe, and decor rooted in Spanish, Mexican, and Native American arts, crafts, and archi-

The naturalistic garden at left is an imaginative marriage of broken concrete and succulents, brought together as if by time and the elements. Below, at the opposite end of the style spectrum, a Tuscany-inspired pergola overlooks a large-scale (and fully functional!) chess set, mixing playful contemporary with more traditional style for an individualistic garden.

OTHER STYLES are more loosely defined; many tend to be interpretations of various period or regional styles, with an emphasis on a particular "mood." A *romantic* or *nostalgic* style—associated with roses, elaborate white furniture, and latticework or picket fences—has elements that blend Victorian with cottage-garden style. *Country* style may conjure up images of split-rail fences, woven-twig chairs, and scarecrows—but it may also include cottage-garden-style flower borders. A *naturalistic* garden is perhaps the most subtle; it's meant to look only lightly touched by human hands, with rocks, logs, and plants arranged to suggest a woodland, desert, meadow, or other natural setting. Here, the ornaments may be special rocks and the plants themselves. *Contemporary* style can be interpreted in a variety of ways. In a *minimalist* garden, a smooth green lawn may stretch out like a carpet under a geometric sculptural shape of gleaming steel, with equally angular plantings like palms or agaves in attendance. But contemporary gardens can also be highly *individualistic* and offbeat: avant-garde, whimsical, or eclectic in style, with ornamentation based on original works of art or assemblages of found objects.

*Diverse elements—
a shingle-roofed
birdhouse, rustic
branch furniture,
picket fencing, and
loads of plant color
and texture—combine
to create an informal
picture of old-
fashioned charm. In
the minimalist garden
shown at right, a more
formal arrangement
features clean lines,
simple forms, and a
subtle palette.*

Defining your own style

Your personal garden style will most likely be
defined by the following elements:
- The architecture of your house
- The ornaments and furnishings you choose
- Your own interpretation of a specific period
  or regional style

    Usually, garden style begins with the home's
architectural character. But style isn't a cast-in-
stone affair; unless you're trying to re-create a
certain period with flawless historical accuracy
or imitate a regional style exclusively, it's most
likely a loose interpretation that you're after.
You'll probably want to select among elements
that evoke the *mood* of a period or region rather
than stick to totally authentic details. A mood
is the ambience that develops when a style is
interpreted in a particular context: for example,
nostalgic or cutting-edge, restful or stimulating,
dignified or playful.

If you live in a grand old residence festooned
with gingerbread trim, a romantic garden featuring white-painted cast-iron furniture and
carriage lamps atop vine-wreathed posts will convey the mood of bygone charm without being
historically accurate. Similarly, if your residence
boasts strikingly contemporary architecture,
selected elements from a Japanese-style
garden—say, moss-covered boulders and simple
bamboo screens—might blend well with the
sleek, strong lines of your home without incorpo-
rating authentic details such as stone lanterns.

    Many styles and themes can be interpreted
either formally or informally, depending on your
taste. An *informal* garden is characterized by a
lack of symmetry and by flowing lines, curves,
natural-looking plant forms, and casual ornaments like found objects or animal figures.
A *formal* one, on the other hand, is typically
symmetrical, featuring straight or geometric
lines, plants trained or clipped into various
shapes (sheared hedges and topiary, for
example), and traditional ornaments such as statuary. A water garden consisting of a rectangular
pool flanked by rows of statues and clipped
shrubs in pots is distinctly formal. If, in contrast,
it featured an irregularly shaped and bordered
pond in a woodland setting, with perhaps a
comical metal frog on a lily pad sculpture, your
water garden would be delightfully informal.

The vignette shown above is the
creation of a unique sensibility:
the designer has arranged
19th-century tools in a parklike
setting to convey old-world
graciousness. At near right,
traditional elements have been
softened into an easy elegance by
leaving shrubs unpruned and
borders undefined. The garden
at top right provides a striking
contrast, with its vivid colors
and bold, distinct plant forms.

the art of design

principles of
composition

ORNAMENTS CAN HELP YOU SHAPE *your garden's space and, almost more than any other element, influence the way you, your family, and friends perceive and experience the garden. They can call attention to a nook that might otherwise be overlooked, or anchor a garden plan by serving as a focal point or centerpiece. They can be delightful elements of surprise that a visitor happens upon while strolling through the garden. The decorative elements you choose can help create your garden's character through their design, color, and texture, as well as through the associations or reactions they evoke. That's why it's important to select ornaments that you really love and then place them where they will make the greatest impact.*

The embodiment of basic design principles of symmetry and harmony, this classic formal garden features paired 18th-century stone figures flanking orderly avenues bordered by neatly trimmed boxwood.

Unity with variety, beautiful colors and textures, careful placement of interesting forms—the well-designed garden at left has it all. Below, a wonderful series of mobile sculptures spans a pond, creating a unified yet provocative landscape.

A sense of unity

Whatever ornaments you use, they will look best if they are part of a unified and harmonious garden design based on principles similar to those for interior decor. In a unified design, the plants, structures, and decorative objects all share one style and character, and all work together to convey the mood of the garden. No one plant, structure, or object stands out too much; rather, all of the the parts work together to establish a sense of *unity*.

The *repetition* of elements such as materials, shapes, and colors helps unify the look and keep it from being a hodgepodge. So, for example, in a serene Japanese-style garden, a single stone lantern set among maple trees will highlight the stone path winding through them—and a bamboo fountain spout trickling water in the foreground will benefit from a backdrop of a simple bamboo fence. In a southwestern garden, a bright blue stucco wall may be visually linked to a series of blue-painted pots arranged across the courtyard, and a tall statue in the center may echo the slim vertical forms of the cacti growing in those pots.

In some gardens (usually formal ones), unity is achieved partly through the use of *symmetry*, with matching elements balanced on either side of a central axis. When these elements are deliberately not matched, the design is *asymmetrical;*

A finely tuned sense of scale is evident in both photos on this page. Above right, a diminutive cherub atop an ornate tiled pedestal looks just right against his backdrop of fine-textured ivy. Below, a massive Japanese temple bell hanging beneath a simple shelter is in keeping with monumental rocks and large-scale plantings.

this characteristic may be found in both formal and informal gardens.

Ornaments in the garden must also be to *scale* if they are to blend attractively. A monumental sculpture will tend to overwhelm a small garden, just as a towering tree will; conversely, a small stone figure will look lost in a spacious setting. Generally, the ornaments you choose should be in proportion to the house, the plantings, and any nearby garden structures. Sometimes you can give a smaller object or statue more importance by placing it atop a pedestal or other support; this will usually look best if the support is surrounded by foliage or flowers that mask the distance between the ground and the ornament. But, of course, some people feel that these rules of scale were made to be broken. If you possess a little boldness and a good sense of design, you may be able to place an oversize statue or other ornament in a small space and make it look wonderful.

Focal points and accents

In a garden, a beautiful or special ornament such as a sculpture, statue, or sundial can become the perfect *focal point*. Whether in a formal or informal setting, a well-chosen focal point provides an almost immediate means of organizing and centering a garden plan. The ornament itself should be on a scale—and of a quality—worthy of notice. Place it where all eyes will be drawn toward it.

In a formal garden, the focal point is often at the end of an *axis*—the centerline of a view or walk. A path, pond, or some other formally delineated line leads the viewer's eye to the object. Landscape elements often align symmetrically on either side of this axis, as in a walkway lined with rows of containers or matching flower beds. In a less formal garden, the axis may be an illusion: a sightline that the brain draws between two significant elements (such as compatible sculptures on either side of a flower bed) rather than one actually laid out.

Sometimes an object becomes a focal point simply by virtue of its anchoring the center of

a circular planting: a handsome sundial in the middle of a classic knot or herb garden, a statue-crowned fountain set at the intersection of several garden paths.

Other ornaments succeed by deliberately ignoring these principles. For instance, an *accent* draws attention to itself by contrasting boldly with its surroundings or by being placed off center—as when a tall, gleaming metal sculpture is set off to one side in an expanse of lawn. Often, strong color alone will suffice to emphasize a single object; imagine, for example, a brightly painted chair resting in a sea of green plantings. Accents add variety and depth to a garden composition or call your attention to a particular spot you want people to notice. They can also draw the gaze *away* from something you don't want seen, such as an unattractive view or utility area.

An axis helps lead the eye to a garden focal point.
At top, a formal path between symmetrical rows of
potted topiaries leads to an ivy-covered bower.
And above, a bronze figure rising dramatically
from the plantings draws the gaze to one end
of an azure pool.

An accent draws attention to itself, sometimes
with bold color, as in the picture at left. Here, a
scattering of bright tiles draws the eye irresistibly to
a wildly original art piece.

displaying
to best effect

T O **S H O W** **O F F** *your treasured ornaments to best advantage you can take several approaches, each with a different effect. Important single pieces can be positioned as focal points in the garden—real attention-getters. Or you can create a sense of discovery by placing ornaments so that they will come as charming surprises to your garden visitors. Smaller objects, especially when they're related in theme, size, color, or use, gain impact when grouped in the garden. Ornaments large and small often acquire substance when given a little extra display height in the form of pedestals or plinths. And don't forget the dramatic possibilities of lighting for showcasing special pieces in the garden.*

The brilliant color of this gate draws you into the scene, enticing you to enter and explore the world within the snow-mantled adobe walls.

The lure of garden ornaments

An effective garden design employs ornaments to help draw you into the scene—to entice you around a corner or down a path to see what's there, or to lead you to a welcoming seat or shelter. With their decorative beauty or the wittiness of their design, ornaments are a natural lure; thoughtful placement will ensure that they will be noticed and fully enjoyed.

Sometimes you'll want to place them where they will be seen immediately. If visitors spot a lovely fountain at the center of a patio, they will probably want to walk over to it and dip their fingers in the splashing water. A beautifully constructed bench set against a mosaic wall hung with vines will beckon anyone to cross over and sit down. And who can resist strolling down a

Little surprises make a garden all the more interesting. At left, angled walls gradually reveal a silvery sheet of water as you round the bend. The lovely sculpted lady below is tucked amid red valerian, awaiting discovery. And the striking ceramic vase shown below left sits half hidden by a tree, where its bright colors will catch the observant eye.

long garden path to inspect the garlanded stone nymph waiting at its end?

On the other hand, don't overlook the elements of mystery and surprise as you ponder placing your ornaments. A large-scale statue or found object partially obscured by foliage extends an irresistible invitation to take a closer look. Likewise, if the splash of water can be heard but not seen, it will seem imperative to discover its source; once found, that fountain or small waterfall will give all the more

pleasure. Planned surprises might include a charming little animal sculpture tucked into a flower bed, a chiseled stone face peeking through foliage, an elaborate birdhouse hanging among trees after a turn in a pathway—all are delightful to encounter.

When grouping pots or garden ornaments, bear in mind the perceptual "rule of three": our brains tend to see three objects as a single unit. So if three pots or three statues are closely correlated in some way—in color, shape, or theme, for example—they will be perceived as a whole and therefore have greater impact. Four objects are usually perceived as two pairs; but if one is larger and more dominant, and the other three closely related to one another, the four together will form a complete visual set.

Where should you place your montage? Anywhere that you want visitors to pause and enjoy, or perhaps in a neglected spot you want to perk up. Larger objects can form a unit on deck or patio, or anchor one side of a short flight of steps. You can place smaller objects on and around a bench or chair, line them up along a windowsill or deck railing, or arrange them on a tabletop. Objects that are light enough may be hung on a wall, a fence, or even a tree. (See page 69 for instructions on how to hang objects.)

Arrayed on a shelf (above) or tucked inside a larger container (below), small pots look charming clustered together. Another grouping (below right) effectively blends various intriguing small-scale objects.

Artful groupings

When you have many smaller ornaments—particularly if they are related in some way to one another—you may want to display them as a group rather than individually, where they might easily be overlooked, seem out of scale, or produce a "spotty" effect. Often you can make use of multiple identical objects, such as matching pots or urns, or small obelisks or pedestals, to help organize space in the garden as well as be decorative in their own right.

More informally, you may want to group a number of unmatched objects to lend them more significance and to create a pleasing vignette. The grouping may comprise a collection of cherished garden objects, such as antique watering cans, birdhouses, animal sculptures—even stones or shells. Or it may be a provocative variety of attractive objects related in color, in texture, in mood, or in style.

Rising to new heights

When you want to give an object special importance in the garden, one surefire method is to elevate it in some way. The standard method for displaying a statue or other important object like an urn is to place it on a pedestal. Pedestals may be obtained from many sources. Ready-made versions cast from stone or concrete are available at garden centers and garden statuary suppliers; older "original" examples, including those made from real stone, can be purchased from building salvage yards, among other sources. You may also find pedestals—antique or new—crafted of wood or metal.

But go beyond the classic pedestal—you can improvise with all sorts of found objects not originally intended as bases. Seek out plant stands made of wirework, cast iron, or other materials suitable for outdoor conditions; bird-baths (ideal for holding gazing balls); large pipes or chimney-flue liners topped with fragments of flagstone or wood; or even, if you're lucky enough to find one, an antique English chimney pot. For an even more casual effect, set a pot or funky art piece atop a sawed-off tree stump or flat-topped boulder. Or stack bricks, tiles, pavers, or flowerpots in an interesting pattern for

a casual pedestal. Whatever you choose for a base, you must make sure it's stable and strong enough to support your display piece. If the object is simply set atop the surface, make sure it doesn't wobble and that it's not where someone could knock it over or the wind topple it. If you are displaying a large, hollow object like an empty oil jar, you might want to weight it by placing a brick or rocks inside for stability. Some improvised pedestals—especially those that aren't in themselves particularly decorative—look best if you plant closely around them, allowing greenery to partially engulf them.

Another form of vertical display is to elevate garden art pieces by hanging them on walls or trees. Sometimes it's enough to tuck a small sculpted piece or found object in the fork of a tree, or in the branches of a shrub or vine climbing against a house wall or fence.

If you want to view small pieces of art from indoors, one idea is to mount a shelf outside a window, with the object or objects affixed to it— or simply set a small, colorful sculpture or figure among plants in a standard window box.

The handsome mosaic urn at left is tall enough to raise its agave plant to spectacular heights.

A stone finial (above) shows to advantage atop a granite pedestal, and the bust of a mysterious lady (left) gains subtle stature on her secluded "pedestal" of branches.

In the inspired pairing
shown above, giant
euphorbias seem to
mimic the lantern's
pointed roof; in
exchange, balancing
the ornament atop
a cairn gives it the
same slightly skewed
angle as the plants.
In the setting below
right, the simple
rounded form of a
handsome urn plays
off the finely detailed
plants around it.

A beautiful partnership

Ideally, plants and garden ornaments should complement and play off one another. Foliage masses and flower borders can act as a backdrop for a sculpture or sundial—or plants and objects may act in concert to create a desired effect. Consider a plant's overall form, leaf shape and texture, and foliage and flower colors when you pair an ornament with it. You may choose plants and ornaments that mirror one another's forms, such as spiky yuccas grouped around a tall, slender abstract sculpture—or you may opt for contrast, gathering those same plants around the pedestal of a round, shiny gazing ball.

Plant leaves and flower textures may be fine or coarse, their structure dainty or bold, their form strap shaped or feathery. Their surfaces may be glossy or matte, fuzzy or slick, bumpy or smooth. Plants with small leaves or leaflets (like lavender and maidenhair fern) and plants with many tiny flowers (like lobelia and 'Moonbeam' coreopsis) are fine textured in appearance. Their best partners will be delicate ornaments or those

with simple, geometric shapes. For drama, choose coarse-textured plants: those with large, bold leaves or flowers. The baroque leaves of bear's breech, the long, pendant flowers of angel's trumpet, or the large, pleated leaves of some hostas are real attention getters. They may either reinforce or contrast with the shapes of your ornaments; but match them to objects with enough presence to stand up to them.

You'll also want to take into account the principles of combining colors (see pages 102–103); be aware, too, that matte-finish plant surfaces will recede a bit visually, whereas glossy or shiny surfaces reflect light and therefore seem to advance. (See the discussion of garden styles on pages 92–97 for more guidance on combining plants with objets d'art.)

In the spotlight

Your garden ornaments need not fade into obscurity at night; in fact, they can become even more dramatic focal points when enhanced by garden lighting techniques. Water features, especially, can look truly magical when given a little night light.

Hidden light fixtures, strategically placed, can be used to good effect. To uplight a statue or sculpture, you place a spotlight at its base, hidden in low-growing foliage, and train it up at

the object. Crosslighting the same object with spotlights from two different points can lend it even more importance. If your object is relatively transparent or open, you can backlight it—uplighting it from behind—to make its outlines glow delicately at night. If an ornament is situated in front of a wall, you have two more options. You can shadowlight it from the front so that its shadow appears on the wall behind, on a dramatically larger scale. Or you can silhouette it, concealing the light source behind it so its black outline shows against a screen of light. Even structures can become ornamental through artistic lighting: if you have a handsomely textured wall, a grazing light mounted to one side, 6 to 8 inches away from the surface, lets the light wash across the wall to create a high-contrast pattern.

Illuminating water features can be as simple as mounting a fixture that will downlight the water from above—often the best choice for a pond featuring fish and plants. But underwater lights, too, can produce dramatic effects, especially on moving water. Waterproof fixtures may be recessed into a concrete pool wall, or be weighted to keep them at the bottom of a pond or in a submerged potted water plant. You can even find lights that float on the water's surface, casting a soft glow as they move about. Some

fountain units come with their own lighting systems, often with optional colored filters. The two types—underwater and surface lighting—can also be combined. For help creating an overall scheme, consult a designer who specializes in garden lighting.

A skillful mixture of lighting techniques lends hushed drama to this nighttime courtyard scene.

ABOVE THE ORDINARY

Pots of trailing flowers and other small treasures often deserve a boost to center stage. But the ornate pedestals sold at garden centers can steal the limelight from the objects they support. This homemade pedestal, made with pressure-treated wood poles available at lumberyards and home centers, has simple lines that allow it to fit attractively into almost any garden space.

Three 4-foot lengths of 5-inch-diameter poles, cut from standard 8-foot poles, form the pedestal; they're connected by 10-inch-long ⅜-inch lag bolts that run through ¾-inch copper pipe couplings.

Viewed from overhead, the pedestal's three poles form an equilateral triangle; together, the pole tops provide a surface wide enough to hold pots as large as 18 inches in diameter.

design credits

FRONT MATTER

1. Design: Marcia Donahue. 4. Design: Mark Henry. 5. Design: Walda Pairon.

CHAPTER ONE/ ARTFUL TOUCHES

7. Design: William Fortington.

A Touch of Whimsy

8 (top left). Design: Gordon Bennett. 8 (bottom). Artist: Charles Smith. 9. Design: Marcia Donahue. 10 (top right). Design: Cindy Morrison/In & Out of the Garden. 10 (bottom). Design: Ewan McKenzie. 11 (top left). Design: Scott Koppes. 12 (bottom left). Design: Elizabeth Berry. 13 (top left). Design: Robert Chittock and Associates. 13 (top right). Design: Robert E. Lee. 13 (bottom left). Design: Suzanne Edison. 13 (bottom right). Design: David Ohashi. 14 (top left). Design: John Roberts Design. 14 (bottom left). Design: Jim Long. 14 (bottom right). Design: Bob Clark. 15 (top left). Artist: Mark Bulwinkle. 15 (bottom left). Design: David Yakish.

15 (right). Design: Françoise Kirkman. 16 (left). Design: Robert Chittock and Associates. 17 (top left). Design: John and Toni Christianson/Christianson's Nursery. 17 (bottom right). Design: Joe and Virginia McDonnal.

Contemporary Treasures

18 (top right). Design: Little and Lewis, Inc. 19. Design: Laura White and Jude Hellewell. 20 (top right). Artist: Bridget McCrum. 20 (bottom left). Artist: Katy McFadden. Design: Barbara Ashmun. 20 (top right). Artist: Bridgett McCrum. 20 (bottom right). Artist: Barbara Hepworth. 21 (top left). Design: Sonny Garcia. 21 (bottom left). Artist: Allen Jones/Roche Court. 21 (bottom right). Artist: Georgia Gerber. 22 (top). Design: Little and Lewis, Inc. 22 (bottom left). Design: Little and Lewis, Inc. 23 (top right). Artist: Carl Dern, Mill Valley Sculpture Gardens. 23 (bottom). Design: Laura White and Jude Hellewell. 23 (top right). Artist: Charles Minor.

The Art of Illusion

25. Design: John Greenlee. 27 (bottom left). Design: Eric Thresher. 27 (bottom right). Design: Sydney Baumgartner.

Classic Ornaments

28 (top right). Design: Mark Henry. 30 (top). Design: Jeff Bale. 31 (bottom right). Design: Thomas Hobbs Designs. 32 (top right). Design: Elspeth Bobbs. 33 (top left). Design: Phil Wood. 33 (top right). Design: Elizabeth Price. 33 (bottom right). Design: Phil Wood.

Ornamental Pots

35. Design: Margie Perry. 37 (top right). Design: Elizabeth Price. 37 (bottom left). Design: Marcia Donahue.

CHAPTER TWO/ ART FROM NATURE

38. Design: Jackie Penney.

The Magic of Water

40 (bottom left). Design: Chris

Jacobson. 42 (bottom). Design: Dick Martin. 43 (top right). Design: Little and Lewis, Inc. 45 (top right). Design: Yugi Koide. 45 (bottom right). Design: Jack Chandler.

Sculpting the Elements

47. Design: Roger Warner. 48 (top left). Design: Ivan Hicks. 48 (bottom right). Design: Sara Stein. 49 (top right). Design: Ann Clark Holt. 49 (bottom right). Design: Mark Henry. 50 (top left). Design: Joe and Virginia McDonnal. 50 (bottom right). Design: Anthony Paul. 50 (bottom left). Design: Jay Knode. 51 (bottom right). Design: Mark Henry. 51 (bottom left). Design: Steve Chase. 52 (left). Design: Laura White and Jude Hellewell. 52 (bottom). Design: Suzanne Porter. 54 (left). Design: Burton Associates. 55 (top right). Design: Steve Martino. 55 (bottom right). Design: Carol Mercer.

Birds in the Garden

56 (top left). Design: B. Leader. 56 (top right). Design: Dan and Darlene Huntington. 58 (bottom left). Artist: Patsy's Pottery. 58 (bottom right). Design: Sara Stein.

CHAPTER THREE/ BEAUTIFUL BASICS

62. Artists: Lidija Tkalcevic, William Wareham. Design: David Schwartz and Associates.

Artful Dividers

64 (top left). Design: Copper Gardens. 64 (bottom right). Design: Bedrock Industries. 65. Design: Michael Schultz. 66 (top left). Artist: Keeyla Meadows. 66 (bottom left). Design: Little and Lewis, Inc. 66 (top right). Design: Diane and Berry Cash. 67 (top left). Design: Mirabel Osler. 67 (bottom left). Design: Mark Bulwinkle. 67 (top right). Artists: Leah Vasquez and Julia Klemek. Design: Jana Ruzicka. 67 (middle right). Design: Topher Delaney. 67 (bottom right). Artist: Keeyla

Meadows. 68 (top). Design: Whithey/Price. 68 (bottom left). Design: M. W. Steele Group Inc. 71. Design: Jeff Bale. 72 (bottom right). Design: Ryan Gainey. 73 (center left). Design: Bobbie Garthwaite. 73 (bottom middle). Design: Bob Clark. 73 (bottom right). Design: Ryl Nowell Wilderness Farm. 74 (top left). Design: Old Rectory, Sudborough, Northants. 74 (bottom right). Design: Sonny Garcia. 74 (center right). Design: Jana Olson Drobinsky. 75 (top). Artist: Keeyla Meadows.

Accent on Furnishings

77. Design: Mark Henry. 78 (top left). Design: Nick Hodges. 78 (bottom left). Design: Michael Schultz. 79 (top left). Design: Richard Wogisch. 79 (top right). Design: Michael Schultz. 80 (top). Design: Roche Court. 80 (center). Design: Di Firth Design. 80 (bottom). Design: Dan Pearson. 81 (top left). Design: Van Atta Associates. 81 (top right). Design: Designs by Ellerie. 81 (bottom right). Design: Lisa Stamm. 81 (bottom left). Design: Margie Perry.

Inviting Retreats

84 (top). Design: Dalton Pavilions, Inc. 84 (bottom right). Design: Freeland Tanner.

The Garden by Night

86 (bottom). Design: Judith Jones. 87. Design: Sonny Garcia. 88 (bottom left). Design: David LeRoy Designs. 88 (bottom right). Design: Joleen and Tony Morales. 88 (top). Design: Topher Delaney. 89 (top left). Design: Brad Eigsti. 89 (bottom left). Design: David LeRoy Designs. 89 (top right). Design: Yugi Koide. 89 (bottom right). Design: Cynthia Del Fava.

CHAPTER FOUR/ THE ART OF DESIGN

A Matter of Style

93 (top). Design: Rofford Manor. 94 (left). Design: Thomas Hobbs Designs. 94 (right). Design:

Henriette Miral. 95 (top). Design: Roger Raiche. 95 (bottom). Design: Jack Chandler. 96 (top). Design: Ryan Gainey. 96 (bottom). Design: Isabelle Greene. 97 (bottom). Artist: Briony Lawson. 97 (top right). Design: Rod Barnett. **Principles of Composition** 99 (top). Design: Little and Lewis, Inc. 99 (bottom). Design: Stone Lane Gardens, Chagford, Devon. 100 (top). Design: Sonny Garcia. 100 (bottom). Design: Terry Welch. 101 (bottom right). Design: Don Morris. 101 (bottom left). Artist: Keeyla Meadows. 102 (bottom). Design: Little and Lewis, Inc. 103 (top). Design: Thomas Hobbs Designs. 103 (bottom). Design: A. Silvestri Co. **Displaying to Best Effect** 105 (top). Design: Laura White and Jude Hellewell. 106 (top). Design: Mirabel Osler. 106 (bottom right). Design: Little and Lewis, Inc. 107 (top left). Design: Margot Knox. 107 (bottom). Design: Marcia Donahue. 108 (top). Design: Jana Olson Drobinsky. 108 (bottom). Design: David LeRoy Designs. 109 (bottom). Design: Peter Whiteley.

PHOTOGRAPHERS

Jean Allsopp©Southern Living, Inc.: 75 center left, 75 bottom middle, 75 bottom right. **David Belda:** 3-3, 34 top left, 40 top left. **Mark Bolton/The Garden Picture Library:** 3-4, 8 top right. **Marion Brenner:** 1, 9, 14 bottom right, 37 bottom left, 47, 74 center right, 107 bottom, 108 top. **Kathleen Brenzel:** 59 bottom right. **Linda Burgess/The Garden Picture Library:** 76 bottom. **Jared Chandler:** 45 bottom right. **Glenn Christiansen:** 67 middle right. **Peter Christiansen:** 51 bottom left. **Connie Coleman:** 94 left, 103 top, 106 bottom left. **Dalton Pavilions, Inc.:** 84 top.

Frederic Didillon/M.A.P.: 21 top right, 42 top left, 54 bottom right. **Derek Fell:** 53 top. **John Glover/The Garden Picture Library:** 3-2, 46 top left, 72 top right, 78 bottom right. **Georgia Glynn-Smith/The Garden Picture Library:** 11 top right, 58 top left. **Steven Gunther:** 54 left, 64 top left. **Mick Hales/GreenWorld Pictures:** 42 bottom, 43 bottom, 48 bottom right, 58 bottom right, 64 bottom left, 72 bottom right, 96 top. **Harry Haralambou:** 3-1, 17 bottom left, 27 top, 31 top right, 32 bottom right, 36 middle left, 38, 43 top left, 48 top right, 55 bottom right, 60 top left, 64 top right, 74 bottom left, 81 bottom right, 92 top. **Lynne Harrison:** 13 bottom left, 14 top left, 17 top right, 18 top right, 21 bottom right, 22 bottom left, 22 top, 31 top left, 31 bottom right, 32 top left, 32 bottom left, 43 top right, 45 bottom left, 49 top left, 49 top right, 49 center left, 51 bottom right, 52 center right, 56 bottom, 58 top right, 58 bottom left, 59 top, 66 bottom left, 68 top, 69 bottom, 77, 78 bottom left, 79 top right, 86 top right, 93 bottom, 99 top, 102 bottom, 106 bottom right. **Sunniva Harte/The Garden Picture Library:** 50 top left, 82 bottom. **Philip Harvey:** 3-6, 4 top, 8 top left, 24 top, 28 top left, 46 bottom left, 58 top left, 68 bottom left. **Saxon Holt:** 6, 40 bottom, 52 bottom, 54 top right, 59 bottom left, 66 top left, 67 bottom right, 75 top, 84 bottom right, 87, 92 bottom, 95 top, 96 bottom, 97 top left, 100 top, back cover. **Dency Kane:** 11 bottom left, 12 top, 36 top left, 78 top right, 85 top right, 101 bottom right, 102 top. **Andrew Lawson:** 2, 8 bottom, 10 top left, 12 bottom right, 16 top right, 20 top left, 20 top right, 20 bottom right, 21 bottom left, 26 bottom, 29, 30 bottom, 31 bottom left, 41, 42 top right, 44 bottom, 45 top left, 46

right, 48 top left, 48 bottom left, 52 top right, 53 bottom left, 55 center left, 55 bottom left, 60 bottom left, 60 bottom right, 66 bottom right, 67 top left, 73 top left, 73 bottom right, 74 top left, 74 top right, 74 bottom right, 79 bottom, 80 top, 80 bottom, 90, 93 top, 97 bottom, 99 bottom, 106 top, 107 top left. **Randy Leffingwell:** 25. **David Duncan Livingston:** 88 top, 109 top. **Allan Mandell:** 15 top left, 20 bottom left, 21 top left, 30 top, 65, 71, 74 center left. **Charles Mann:** 11 bottom right, 12 bottom left, 13 top right, 14 bottom left, 22 bottom right, 23 top left, 27 bottom left, 32 top right, 35, 44 top left, 55 top right, 66 top right, 67 bottom left, 73 bottom middle, 81 bottom left, 84 bottom left, 98 top, 104 bottom, 105 bottom left, 105 bottom right. **David McDonald/PhotoGarden, Inc.:** 4, 10 top right, 10 bottom, 11 top left, 13 top left, 13 bottom right, 15 bottom left, 16 left, 17 top left, 17 bottom right, 19, 23 bottom, 23 top right, 28 bottom left, 28 top right, 33 top left, 33 top right, 33 bottom right, 37 top right, 45 top right, 49 bottom right, 50 top right, 50 bottom left, 52 left, 56 top right, 62, 64 bottom right, 69 top, 70 top left, 73 center left, 81 top right, 86 bottom left, 88 bottom left, 88 bottom right, 89 top left, 89 bottom left, 89 top right, 105 top, 108 bottom, 111. **Keeyla Meadows:** 101 bottom left. **Ncum/M.A.P.:** 53 bottom right. **N. et P. Mioulane/M.A.P.:** 34 bottom, 36 bottom right. **Marie O'Hara/The Garden Picture Library:** 37 bottom right. **Hugh Palmer:** 18 top left, 18 bottom left, 36 top right, 40 top right, 60 top right, 76 top, 107 right. **Michael Paul/The Garden Picture Library:** 50 bottom right. **Jerry Pavia:** 85 bottom left. **Norman A. Plate:** 3-5, 7, 15 right, 67 top right, 79 top left, 89 bottom right, 95 bottom. **Rob**

Proctor: 44 top right. **Richard Rethemeyer:** 63. **Howard Rice/The Garden Picture Library:** 37 top left, 61, 70 bottom left. **Susan A. Roth:** 82 top. **A. Silvestri Co.:** 103 bottom. **J. S. Sira/The Garden Picture Library:** 16 bottom right, 78 top left, 98 bottom, 101 top. **Janet Sorrell/The Garden Picture Library:** 24 bottom. **Sean Sullivan:** 86 top left, 91. **Ron Sutherland/The Garden Picture Library:** 26 top, 72 bottom left, 73 top left, 83, 85 bottom right. **Brigitte Thomas/The Garden Picture Library:** 5. **Michael S. Thompson:** 34 top right, 68 bottom right, 69 bottom left, 70 right, 84 center left, 85 top left, 100 bottom, 110. **Deidra Walpole Photography:** 14 top right, 27 bottom right, 57, 72 top left, 81 top left, 104 top. **Virginia Weiler:** 94 right. **Peter O. Whiteley:** 109 bottom. **Tom Woodward:** 39. **Steven Wooster/The Garden Picture Library:** 51 top, 73 top right, 80 center, 97 top right.

index